Natural Relations

The natural world offers many health benefits.
Connecting with nature allows an inner peace, a calm which awakens a fuller relationship with our potential.
Nature assists us because our body is nature.

Light opens life.

Sunrise is new light allowing fresh possibilities.

Food gives strength.

*A vast variety of
nourishment is available
throughout our world.*

*Our earth is composed of
all we are made of,
and all we require.*

*May we greet all of life with
respect, gratitude,*

patience, and wonder.

Beauty is all around.

*Nature uses change
to blend all
into harmony.*

*Otter is playfully creative,
always finding how to flow happily
with whatever life presents.
Otter acts by taking care
of self first while
ensuring to care for others
as well.*

Enchanting events
can take our breath away.

Breathe, enjoy the feelings,
as we center our self

in the charming energy.

Observe life.

Awareness gives understanding
while improving our options.

An oar steadies a boat.

Breath steadies and strengthens us.

Splashing is OK!

Honor life's vitality
when gusto emerges.

Harmony is beautiful.

Vibrational patterns
in all forms of harmony;
light, music, or,
in the body,

display beauty and health.

Nestlings emerge from their eggs,
Red shouldered hawk
instantly flies out
into an open area to sing proudly.

Sing & rejoice

as our efforts prosper life.

Smile into heart,
breathe to deepen relaxation,
& enable the fullness
of a journey's gifts to appear.

*Nectar transports us
into experiencing
the wonderful light
and love of oneness.*

Surprise awakens our curiosity.

Soar.
Ride life's journey.
Adjust, blend into change.

Grow trust.

Moon rides pink dragon.

As moon waxes,
grows towards fullness,
it increases it's power to lift
the ocean's tides,
and our aspirations.

A pink dragon is a primal force
for protection of innocence,
health and pure love.

Appreciate now.
The tide is out. Birds alight for a
temporary respite. Now, life is gentle.
Enjoy such time. The tide will return
to cover this place.

Life's adventure is filled with variety.
Let us enjoy our choices as we meet
each day's opportunity
to perform our potential.

Notes

These pictures were taken on a journey to refresh myself by being immersed in nature. For 9 months, I oriented towards pleasant weather, and interesting estuaries in which I was able to row Sapphire, my 14' boat. Birds, otter, waterways, trees, and sky were among the natural relations I learned from.

In Gratitude,
John W. Cardano

Other books by John Cardano

THE FABRIC OF HEALTH

The Fabric of Health is a venture to express the dimensions that weave life. Mind, spirit, and body are all involved.

LITTLE WILD HORSE CANYON

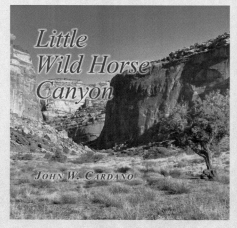

Little Wild Horse Canyon is a picture book for all ages, it's poem unites wind and breath as forces of nature shaping the landscape and our health.

Printed in the United States
By Bookmasters